A PLAY IN ONE ACT

O. HENRY'S

The Cop and the Anthem

adapted for the stage

by

MARK BUCCI

THE DRAMATIC PUBLISHING COMPANY

Printed in the United States of America

(THE COP AND THE ANTHEM)

for Dorothy Bachmann

THE COP AND THE ANTHEM

A Play in One Act

For Five Men and Eight Women*

CHARACTERS

(In order of appearance)

LEMUEL T. THWACKBUSHER
HEAD WAITRESS
SALESLADY
STREET CLEANER
TOUGH BOY
MAN WITH UMBRELLA
MOTHER
LITTLE GIRL
TWO WOMEN
FLORABELLE
OLD LADY
COP(S)

PLACE: New York City.

TIME: Just before winter, 1908.

---

*More or less, as desired. See Production Notes, page 33.

The Cop and the Anthem

LEMUEL T. THWACKBUSHER, a somewhat seedy-looking man of indeterminate age, is lying on a park bench, a newspaper blanketing him against the chilly evening. A few leaves have fallen on the bench; one is perched on his nose. He stirs, takes hold of the leaf and rises to a seated position, achieving some degree of tatty dignity. (NOTE: This role may be played like W. C. Fields, or not.)

LEMUEL (looking at the leaf). Ah, yes, one of those annual calling cards. It says--("Reading" the leaf.)--"When wild geese honk high in the night and when women without fur coats grow kind to their husbands, then, Lemuel T. Thwackbusher, make ready to leave your park bench, for the rigors of winter are upon you. Sincerely yours, Jack Frost." (He wryly tosses the leaf aside and, stirring uneasily, fiddles with his newspaper blanket.) All right, where to? A Mediterranean cruise . . . drifting in the Vesuvian Bay? Lolling under Florida skies? Or perhaps South America? (A brief Latin pose, arms up, fingers snapping.) But every year at this time, I consider how "gauche" it would be to follow the "nouveau riche" on their ostentatious trips planned to impress one another. And every year I look forward to my favorite winter resort, right here in New York. Ah, yes, Blackwell's Island. Some call it a prison, but to me it's three months of bed and board, safe from the two things that mar this otherwise perfect city; namely the winter cold and the police. (Somewhat conspiratorial.) But the Law is an integral part of my yearly plan, for since the police are ever anxious to make arrests and judges determined to pass sentence, all I do is commit a simple misdemeanor and afford them the eager pursuit of their duties. *Voilà,* in a trice, I'm *vvv* booked for three months on Blackwell's Island. No travel bureau could provide faster service! (Gets up, starts folding newspaper.)

And the best part is that my self-esteem remains unsullied. For by a simple arrest, I earn my winter vacation. No charity ward for Lemuel T. Thwackbusher. Besides, the Law is more benign than Philanthropy. The gifts of municipal charity are paid for in humiliation of spirit. (Throughout the following, he takes a short cigar butt from his jacket and, sticking a toothpick through it as a cigar holder, lights it.) As Caesar had his Brutus, every loaf of bread has its compensation of personal inquisition and every charity bed its toll of a bath. Obviously it's better to be a guest of the Law which, though conducted by rules, doesn't meddle unduly with a gentleman's private affairs. (He puts the newspaper on the bench and rolls the bench completely offstage R.)

Now then, how do I get arrested? The pleasantest way is to dine luxuriously at some expensive restaurant, and after declaring insolvency, be handed over quietly to a policeman. An accommodating magistrate will do the rest.

(He walks slowly in a broad circle, as if sauntering into a more elegant neighborhood.)

LEMUEL (briefly feeling his chin). Clean-shaven, decent coat--(Fingering his tie.)--and this barely used gift from the Salvation Army. (Looks down at pants, which are a bit the worse for wear.) If I could be seated quickly, my top half might give a reasonable impression of affluence. A brief look at the menu and I'll order a roasted mallard duck, with a bottle of Chablis. And then Camembert, a demi-tasse and a cigar. Such a small repast won't provoke undue revenge from the management; yet it will leave me filled and happy for the journey to my winter refuge. Three months on Blackwell's Island!

(A HEAD WAITRESS, a formidable and imposing woman bristling with frosty hauteur, comes forth stage L, reservation tablet in one hand. In the other, she carries a tall potted plant, placing it left of C, and stands downstage of it. Possibly there's some tepid trio music playing softly in the background. Smoothly approaching this area, LEMUEL removes his hat, mimes entering this elegant restaurant, and approaches the HEAD WAITRESS.)

HEAD WAITRESS (barely looking up from tablet). You have a reservation?

LEMUEL (hadn't anticipated this). Ah, yes, a reservation . . .

HEAD WAITRESS (firmly). The name, please.

LEMUEL. Uh . . . Lemuel T. Thwackbusher. (As HEAD WAITRESS checks lists.) The T. is for Theodosius, in honor of my maternal grandfather. Poor man was killed in the flood of '79.

HEAD WAITRESS (staring at list, with contemptuous

surprise). You have no reservation.

LEMUEL. Done in by an excess of water.

HEAD WAITRESS (looking at LEMUEL fully for the first time). Who are you . . .

LEMUEL (aside, unheard by her). Apparently hard of hearing.

HEAD WAITRESS. . . . that you feel you can be served in a restaurant such as "Bombazine's," let alone be seated. Look at you! Frayed cuffs, ill-fitting--(Nose-wrinkling smirk.)--clothes . . . and those shoes. (LEMUEL hastily rubs his right shoe against his left pant leg.)

LEMUEL (a bit defensive). Genuine alligator, madam. A gift from a lady missionary!

HEAD WAITRESS (pointing). Out!

LEMUEL. I was prepared to give you ample retribution, I mean restitution, for a meal here . . .

HEAD WAITRESS (grabbing him by the collar). Out!

LEMUEL. . . . but under the circumstances, I've decided to go . . .

HEAD WAITRESS (pushing him right of their playing area). Out!

LEMUEL (after he collapses in a heap) . . . elsewhere! (The HEAD WAITRESS quickly turns, casts her eyes heavenward, picks up the potted plant and goes off L. LEMUEL gets up and brushes himself off, nursing his bruised dignity.) Cantankerous churl ought to be arrested for felonious assault! (Moves to another area.) Well, it seems this year my route to Blackwell's Island will not be an epicurean one. (Thinks.) What other way is there of entering that gentle limbo?

(A prim, middle-aged SALESLADY has entered R, rolling on a counter which she positions at RC. On the counter are several assorted boxes of candies, elegantly packaged bob-bons, dried fruits, etc. A COP saunters on to LC area;

seeing him, LEMUEL looks R and sniffs the air.)

LEMUEL. Ah, a confectionery establishment. Perhaps a minor theft will pave my way with bonbons. (He approaches the area RC.) A figure of speech, for I hate candy. (As he mimes entering the candy shop, we hear the tinkling door bell.)

SALESLADY (her manner brusque and efficient). Good evening, sir. May I help you?

LEMUEL (quickly checking to see that the COP is near by). Uh, yes. (He approaches the counter, trying to appear casual.) Nothing elaborate. Ah, do you mind if I look around?

SALESLADY. Of course not. (LEMUEL goes through a detailed scrutiny of different candy boxes, checking the weight of one, sniffing another, admiring a bow, etc., ad infinitum, but since she's suspicious of him, she remains there staunchly observing him. She checks the timepiece pinned to her blouse.) I'd like to indicate to you that the store closes in eight minutes.

LEMUEL. In that case, you must have things to do preparatory to closing shop.

SALESLADY (pointedly). My first obligation is to the customer. (Picks up a candy box.) Would these chocolate creams be of interest? They're filled with assorted flavors from Cuban vanilla to raspberries shipped from Troy, N.Y.

LEMUEL (a face). Er, no . . .

SALESLADY (another box). These after-dinner mints are quite good. They're made from sweet butter and fresh mint from South Carolina.

LEMUEL (dismissing these with a wry fabrication). Yes, they serve those at the Maison Dixon. I had stomach cramps for three days.

SALESLADY (regarding a fancy basket). This item is very popular for someone going on a trip. Besides the dried fruit such as dates and figs, it has a wide assortment of confections. Is the gift for someone who is leaving?

LEMUEL (giving her a look). Well, not exactly.

SALESLADY. I don't wish to appear nosy, but if I knew for whom the gift was meant, I might be able to help you . . . make up your mind.

LEMUEL (would so like to be rid of her). It's difficult to decide, knowing I'm keeping you from your duties.

SALESLADY (pressing on). Is the gift for a young person graduating from one of our higher academies of learning?

LEMUEL (aside, unheard by her). I'd sooner give them a funeral wreath!

SALESLADY. Or perhaps a birthday memento for someone, a friend . . .

LEMUEL (mumbling in his fury). No. . . .

SALESLADY. . . . or a member of the family?

LEMUEL (to himself). Holy Mother! (The SALESLADY hears the last word.)

SALESLADY (stopping, her lower lip suddenly trembling). Your . . . mother?

LEMUEL (exasperatedly dissembling). Yes, it's for my mother. (The SALESLADY snatches a handkerchief from her blouse's cuff and momentarily holds it to her mouth, for she is barely able to contain the flood of tears which is to follow.)

SALESLADY. Excuse me. (She runs of R, starting to cry. At first LEMUEL is perplexed. But who cares, he's gotten rid of her.)

LEMUEL (gingerly picking up the basket). Of course somebody's going on a trip. I am! (With an elaborate display of stealth, he takes the basket to the door, which he mimes opening several times, making sure the door's tinkling bell is heard. And standing there moving the door repeatedly, he not only looks R, but more toward the COP L, whose attention he's trying to get. When he's satisfied he has, LEMUEL broadly and slowly sneaks out of the shop. Seeing this, the COP runs up to him and grabs him by the arm. LEMUEL, with exaggerated disappointment:) Oh, drat! Drat! Caught red-handed! Ah, there's no trying to put anything over on the Law. Right there in the nick of time. (Ad libs yessir, etc.)

(Simultaneously the SALESLADY has returned R, behind the counter, with a large ready-made bow in hand. Not finding LEMUEL in the shop, she cranes her head past the door and sees the COP about to make an arrest.)

SALESLADY (shouting to the COP). No, wait! (She runs out of the shop. To COP.) What are you doing to this man! (The COP mimes surprise and confusion.) Let go of him, do you hear!

LEMUEL (aside). Madam, let him do his duty.

SALESLADY (furiously, to COP). How dare you harass innocent people! Are the streets now to be unsafe from the defenders of the Law?

LEMUEL. Madam, please . . .

SALESLADY (hitting the COP). Begone! Go elsewhere and catch criminals, if you know what they look like! (The COP hastens away, exiting L.) And leave upstanding citizens alone!

LEMUEL (after a thwarted beat). But, madam, I'm guilty.

SALESLADY (now brimming with effusive sympathy). Guilty? Yes. Guilty of risking incarceration so that you might give your mother a gift. Guilty of losing your civil honor so that she would know you think of her. (He tries to talk, but she puts her hand up.) I know you don't have money to pay for it. But such an open-hearted, self-sacrificing gesture must not go unrewarded. Take your present to your mom. Is it her birthday? (LEMUEL shakes his head "no.") Is she . . . sick? (He's too confused to find an answer and merely shrugs his shoulders, which the SALESLADY interprets as "yes." She puts her hand on his arm in pained empathy and briefly squeezes it.) I know what you're going through. I . . . lost my mother early this year. (Close to tears again.) She had so much to live for . . .

LEMUEL (trying his best to feign sympathy). Nipped in her prime, eh?

SALESLADY (nods, fighting back the tears). She was ninety-seven! (LEMUEL balefully looks front. Then brushing aside a tear, the SALESLADY puts the large bow on the basket.) Now then, go and be the good son--I know you are--and brighten up your mother's day.

LEMUEL (holding the basket like a dead albatross). But I stole it!

SALESLADY (starts going into shop). Knowing of your goodness is payment enough.

LEMUEL. But I . . .

SALESLADY (tearfully inspirational). May heaven protect all your days. (The door tinkles closed, and she nobly goes off R, pushing the candy counter with her. Left alone, all LEMUEL can do is look out front with an expression of crushing irony.)

LEMUEL (after a pause, quietly). Oh, how I hate

candy.

(From UR a uniformed, mustached STREET CLEANER walks on, tugging an old fashioned, round, two-wheeled trash cart behind him with one hand. In the other he holds a street-cleaning broom against his shoulder. He saunters lackadaisically across the stage, singing "The Streets of New York" to himself, and passes in front of LEMUEL. Though the two men ignore each other, LEMUEL's expression clearly shows what he thinks of the man's singing. Just as the street cleaner is about to go off L, LEMUEL gets an idea and shoots the candy basket into the trash cart like an expert basketball player. The STREET CLEANER exits L, unaware of the point scored.)

LEMUEL. So much for saccharine sentimentality. (Starts moving to another spot.) Now . . . what other way can I get to Blackwell's Island? (Thinks, then gets a distressing thought.) Gadzooks, am I losing my touch?

(The outline of a store window appears UL [pushed on by a pole].)

LEMUEL (turning, sees window). Of course not! (He mimes looking for and picking up a rock. Then, winding up for a terrific pitch, he mimes hurling it at the window. If the sound of shattering glass is inconvenient, then a sign reading "crash!" is flipped down from the upper parallel strut [released offstage by a string] and LEMUEL looks R and L.) Where's a cop? (Waits impatiently, looks some more.) When you need them, they're never around!

(A TOUGH BOY enters front DL. He wears a cap, moth-eaten sweater and knickers, and is bouncing a ball. He ignores LEMUEL as he starts walking R.)

LEMUEL (seeing the BOY). Go 'way, boy, you bother me. (The BOY stops DR and, hands on hips, shoots LEMUEL a defiant gesture of the head.)
BOY. Yah!

(A COP runs on from UR, going directly to LEMUEL and the window. NOTE: This time the cop is a Swede, with a blond mustache, and possibly blond hair showing from under his hat.)

COP (with a Swedish accent). Yust a minute. Who did that?
LEMUEL (serenely smiling). Don't you think I might've had something to do with it?
COP. Men who break vindows don't stay to talk vith policeman. They run away. (The COP glances at the BOY, who does a take.) Yew! (You!) (Having been the victim of injustice too often, the BOY knows better than to try and explain.)
BOY. Yipe! (And dashes off R.)
COP (in hot pursuit). Come back here, yew! Py yumpin' yiminy, don't yew know it's a crime to break vindows. Stop, stop in the name of the Law! (The COP is already off R.)
LEMUEL (after a grim look front). Is Blackwell's Island to be an unattainable Arcadia this year? Why are there so many obstacles to my haven in the harbor? (We hear the wind blowing, and he shudders.) Blast you, Jack Frost, your calling card was more than specific. (Beats his upper arms against the cold.) I got the

message! (He walks a bit, mumbling to himself.) Dad rat it. Victim of cruel circumstances.

(A well-dressed MAN walks on and stops facing forward at extreme DR, placing a stand sign reading "trolley stop" to his left. Then he leans his umbrella against the sign and starts reading the newspaper which was tucked under his arm. He's obviously waiting for a trolley. LEMUEL glances at the man, then cranes further, noticing the umbrella.)

LEMUEL (aside). Perhaps another attempt at larceny. "Petit" larceny. (LEMUEL goes behind the MAN, takes the umbrella, moves right of him, making a pointed display of having committed the theft by slowly sneaking away. The MAN notices him.)

MAN. Hold on there, that's my umbrella.

LEMUEL (defiantly). Oh, is it now!

MAN (grabbing it from LEMUEL). Yes, it is!

LEMUEL (forcibly retrieving it). And I say it's mine!

MAN. If by that you mean possession is nine-tenths of the Law, let me advise you that you came by that umbrella illegally, for I distinctly saw you try to purloin it just now!

LEMUEL. Indeed? Well, why don't you call a policeman? I took it. Your umbrella. Why don't you call a cop? (Looks R.) Look, there's one down at the next corner.

MAN. Of course. (But he hesitates.)

LEMUEL. I'll get him.

MAN (restraining him). Hold on, there.

LEMUEL. Sir, if your sense of justice is offended, defend it!

MAN (still restraining him). Of course . . . but . . .

uh . . .

LEMUEL. What's right is right.

MAN. Yes . . . that is . . . well, you know how these mistakes occur----I--if it's your umbrella, I hope you'll excuse me . . .

LEMUEL (fearing the worst). What?

MAN. You see, I picked it up this morning in a cigar shop. If you recognize it as yours, why--I hope you'll take it back with no hard feelings. And I trust you'll be generous enough not to call that policeman and press charges. I mean, nobody wants to get in touble with the Law . . .

LEMUEL (to himself, an ironic semi-laugh). Huh-huh . . .

MAN. So you'll do me a great favor if you'll behave like the gentleman I know you must be, from the extremely good styling of this umbrella, and accept my sincere apologies for this gross oversight. To err is human, to forgive divine. (A trolley bell is heard.) And now, I bid you adieu, sir, for I'll miss my trolley. (Taking the sign with him, he scampers off L, index finger pointing upward.) Ho there! Ho!

LEMUEL (after a pause). Has it come to this . . . Lemuel T. Thwackbusher can't get arrested?. . . (Using the umbrella like a cane, he starts walking. Suddenly there is the sound of surging wind and the umbrella snaps open horizontally, caught in a gust [use self-opening umbrella for this]. Against his will, LEMUEL is pulled clear across to UR by the umbrella. He furiously turns, facing the wind with the umbrella before him, trying to close it as he struggles against the unseen tide.) Blasted investion of the devil! (Gaining headway, he works diagonally back to DL, when another gust catches him off guard, spinning him back again.)

(THREE WOMEN and a little GIRL enter UL. Upon seeing LEMUEL, they stop, and despite themselves, gradually are amused by him. After a few more comic turns, LEMUEL falls, grabbing the open umbrella as if it were a wild beast which he has succeeded in quelling. Seated on the ground, he closes it.)

LITTLE GIRL. What's that man doing, Mamma?
MOTHER. Nothing, child. (Briefly putting her hands over the girl's ears, to WOMAN ONE.) I think he's fighting the demon rum! (But sanctimonious curiosity wins over parental concern, and as if by her silent command, they all remain to watch him.)
LEMUEL (having sized up the situation; aside to audience). Ah! Perhaps a disorderly conduct charge! (He leaps up, assuming a fencer's stance with the closed umbrella.) All right, Jack Frost! Try to wreck my priceless parapluie? . . . Avaunt, foul foe, you've met your match. En garde! (He goes through a drunken duel with his invisible foe, the parries and thrusts accompanied by near-shouts.) Back, back, I say, to the tundra made barren by your paper rain! Slash your rapier chill at mountains of ice, not creatures of the sun! (Another thrust.) Take that, you frozen burp!
LITTLE GIRL. He's funny, Mamma.
MOTHER. Hush, child.
LEMUEL (thrust). Hah! (Thrust.) Hah! (Suddenly screams, holds his shoulder and drops back.) Ah . . . wounded . . . by a windy icicle. (Garners strength again.) All right, I'll get you. (Looks about.) Where are you? Come on,

fight like a man. (As he calls, he turns slowly, back to audience.) Ho, there . . . ho . . . ho . . . ho . . . (There is a total change of character as he completes his turn, facing front. Using the umbrella for a vaudevillian's cane, he bursts into unaccompanied song.)
Oh----
Won't you come home, Bill Bailey?
Won't you come home?
She'd cry the whole day long.
(Improvising dance steps and bits throughout.)
I'll do the cookin', darlin',
I'll pay the rent.
I know I've done you wrong.

(A COP walks on R, going to the group at stage L. NOTE: This time the cop is Irish, with rosy cheeks and nose. Seeing the COP, LEMUEL becomes more exaggerated in his routine.)

LEMUEL. 'Member that rainy eve when
I threw you out . . .
(The feminine GROUP and the COP can't help laughing at him.)
With nothin' but a fine-tooth comb.

WOMAN TWO (though amused, feels she must show her civic concern to the COP). Officer, what is the world coming to? (LEMUEL has stopped, eagerly anticipating arrest.)

COP (with a brogue). Oh, think nuthin' of it, ma'am. 'Tis one of them Yale lads bein' initiated to a fraternity. Hazin', I think they call it.

LEMUEL (dropping down on both knees, continuing more loudly).
I know I'm to blame . . .
(No desired response from the COP who, along with the feminine GROUP, starts sauntering R.)

Well, ain't that a shame . . .

COP. Noisy, but no harm.

LEMUEL (moving after them on both knees, hands clasped before him).

Bill Bailey, won't you please . . .

WOMAN ONE. I thought he was--(Tabu word.)--Intoxicated!

LEMUEL (pleading, extending the song by one phrase).

Or else I'm gonna freeze . . .

COP. No, ma'am, it's all right. We've instructions to lave them be.

LEMUEL (desperate). Bill Bailey, won't you please . . .

LITTLE GIRL (as she exits R). Mamma, what does "innoxitated" mean?

MOTHER (sharply, as she follows off). Never mind. Where did you hear such a word! (The COP and the GROUP are gone. LEMUEL is left alone on his knees at extreme R, and seems to deflate with discouragement.)

LEMUEL (paraphrasing the song's finish, he speaks the last two words with an accompanying "go 'way" gesture). Go home! (He gets up, brushes off his trouser knees, and straightening his jacket, tries to regain some dignity. Umbrella by his left side, he stands tall, as if scanning the horizon for some clue to his dilemma. He smooths out his jacket and tie with his right hand.) If I can just collect my thoughts, I'm sure the answer will come to me. (Suddenly there's a gust of wind. The umbrella in his left hand snaps open and out horizontally, carrying him clear across the stage.) Aaaaaar-rrrggghhh! (He is catapulted off L and we hear the crashing and clanging of garbage cans, the angry squeal of a cat, possibly glass shattering and LEMUEL's furious and helpless cries.

There is another gust of wind.)

(Presently LEMUEL stalks on fighting a large newspaper sheet which the wind's force and his hasty walk keep close to his face and torso. [NOTE: He's abandoned the umbrella offstage.] He finally takes one corner of the newspaper between thumb and forefingers of one hand and peels off the paper just as the wind subsides. Triumphantly looking at it, he tries to throw the paper away to one side. But some gummy substance from the garbage must have gotten on his gloves and/or the newspaper, for the paper refuses to leave his fingers. Again he tries to throw it away, and again it remains. He does this a few times, with typical W. C. Fields reactions building from "oh well, that's taken care of" to "egad, I'm tied to a millstone!"

Then, he carefully manages to transfer the newspaper to the thumb and forefinger of his other hand and tries to throw it away. But the recalcitrant paper refuses to leave this hand, too, with a further build of reactions from LEMUEL with each futile attempt. It's as if the paper were demanding to be read. A printed item catches his eye. Now holding the paper with both hands by its two furthermost top ends, LEMUEL looks closer at it.)

LEMUEL (reading). "Tomorrow's weather: cloudy and colder, possibility of snow!" Aaarrgghh. (He tries to throw the paper away, but now he's stuck to it with both hands. He frantically waves it hither and yon; now looking like a housewife airing linen, now like a matador barely being missed by the bull.

Desperately trying to figure out the puzzle, he decides to transfer one end of the paper to the other hand, so that at least only one hand will be affected. He does this slowly and carefully, anticipating success. For now that the two ends of the paper are between the thumb and forefinger of one hand, perhaps the new, and thusly concentrated distribution of the paper's weight will better respond to his efforts.

But try though he may, it doesn't work. He twirls about, insanely snapping the paper like some obdurate thermometer. In a rage, he stops, looks at the ground and the paper and comes to a decision. He places the paper on the ground and puts a foot on the cornered areas near his fingers. Ever so carefully he pulls his fingers away from the paper [standing with one foot on the paper]. Success! Beaming, he looks at one hand, then the other. He's free at last and brushes his hands off in self-satisfaction. But as he starts to walk away, the newspaper is now stuck to his shoe [either use double-faced adhesive on the shoe's edge, or mime being rooted in place].)

LEMUEL (exploding). Bad news! (In a paroxysm of rage, he attacks the paper, rolling about on the ground as he tears it to pieces, pushing most of them past the footlights off the stage. One medium-sized piece of the newspaper remains to catch his eye, and he picks it up.)

LEMUEL (reading). "City concerned over increase in 'mashers'" . . . "Accosting of women on the streets by those of the opposite gender becoming a problem." . . ."'Police have been alerted,' says Commissioner McCloskey." (Thinks.) Hmmmmm . . . masher . . . (Gets up, throws paper away, walks about a bit.) My back is against the wall. A chilly blindfold is being placed over my eyes . . . and winter's firing squad is taking aim. (A plea.) Though I fain would not besmirch the sensibilities of any member of the feminine denomination, do I have any other recourse? Masher, it will be.

(The outline of a store window [same one as before] is pushed on extreme DL. [Across the front, it might have lettering on a transparent background reading "millinery" seen in reverse by the audience.] Simultaneously a very attractive and apparently refined WOMAN enters R and saunters over to the shop window, before which she stops and casually looks into it [i.e., out toward the audience]. She is elegantly dressed and wears a large picture hat. Toward the end of this transition, a COP enters extreme UL, walks to UR and stops facing front, billy club held down before him in both hands. NOTE: This COP is Italian, with a dark mustache and dark hair showing from under his hat.

This is a perfect set-up for LEMUEL and with a "well, it has to be done" shrug, he assumes the masher role. Briefly checking his sartorial elegance, he pulls out another short cigar butt, sticks a toothpick through it and lights up. Then tilting his hat at a rakish angle, he approaches the woman and stops a few feet near her, pretending to look in the shop window. Though the COP is aware of what's going on, he does nothing for the present.

LEMUEL clears his throat -- the woman remains impassive. He coughs lightly -- ditto. He takes a puff of his cigar, but inadvertently has a coughing spasm. Wiping his eyes, he returns to normal and disappointedly sees the woman still has taken no notice of him. The COP has, however, and takes a few steps in their direction. LEMUEL moves a step closer to the woman -- still no reaction. Inclining his head in her direction, he wiggles his eyebrows at her. Still, nothing.

Finally, LEMUEL doffs his hat to her and speaks in as lecherous a tone as he can affect.)

LEMUEL. Ah, there, Bedelia! Do you want to come and play in my yard? (The woman turns pleasantly to him and her voice and manner have a mellifluous, over-seductive quality. NOTE: This roll may be played like Mae West, or not.)

WOMAN. Of course, if you'll treat me to some champagne along the way. (LEMUEL's jaw drops.) I'd've spoken to you sooner, but the "gendarme" was watching. (LEMUEL can only stare in consternation. The COP crosses diagonally to them as the woman puts her arm in LEMUEL's, crossing C.)

COP (Italian accent). Excusa me, signorina, isa that man bother you?

WOMAN (dissembling). Gracious no, officer. Doctor Clangwell is an old friend of the family and distantly related by the recent marriage of my cousin Eustacia.

COP. Oh, HO.K. (Starts to exit L.) Buta you know, you nunja cana be too carefu'.

WOMAN (waving him off). I know, a girl just isn't safe nowadays. (The COP has exited L. The WOMAN turns to LEMUEL.) I was afraid the evening was going to be dull, but fortuitously you interrupted my reverie.

LEMUEL (stammering). Well -- uh----

WOMAN. Now, what was that you said about champagne?

LEMUEL. Well, actually, miss, there's been some mistake . . .

WOMAN (calmly). Mistake?

LEMUEL. Well, yes, in a way . . . You see . . .

WOMAN. Don't worry about it. You're just . . . shy. And I've never met a shy man I didn't like. Now, where shall we go -- Rector's? Tony Pastor's?

LEMUEL. Uh . . . Well . . .

WOMAN. How about Bombazine's?

LEMUEL (does a take). The place is a menace to public health.

WOMAN. Well, since you're obviously a man of decision, I leave the choice entirely in your capable hands.

LEMUEL. The fact of the matter is, you're preventing me from leaving on an important . . . expedition.

WOMAN. Oh, a man of destiny.

LEMUEL. Yes, anthropological work in Bucaramanga; I'll be gone at least three months.

WOMAN. Well, I've never been one to thwart a man with a mission. (Pleasantly disengaging herself from him, gradually moving R.) Besides, I can't wait that long . . . By the way, my name's Florabelle Hobbs and I'm staying at the Chelsea. (Stops extreme R and turns to him.) When you get back, come up and . . . renew the acquaintanceship. (As she exits R, the shop window is pulled off L.)

LEMUEL (a glance heavenward, then distraught). Is nothing sacred? What's happened to Law and Order? Has its once sturdy framework collapsed around deaf ears? The fall of the Roman Empire was but a "tea dansante" compared to what's happening in this city. O justice, justice! Uncover your eyes, drop those rusty pie pans and look at me! I'm freezing and I wish you'd let me get to Blackwell's Island!

(An old, OLD LADY, almost an exaggerated crone, hobbles on from R, shrouded from head to foot in an all-covering, amorphous garment. In her hands she holds a tray which is further supported by a cord tied to its two outer corners and looped around her neck. The open tray contains a variety of home-made items: boxes of matches, pot-holders, artificial flowers, carved wooden figurines, candles, etc. etc. Since poverty has always nipped at her heels, her movements are quick and furtive, and her voice has an urgent, raspy precipitousness. Spotting LEMUEL, she makes a beeline for him and tugs his sleeve.)

OLD LADY. Need some matches, mister?

LEMUEL (hadn't seen her coming, emits a startled sound). Hu-u-uh!

OLD LADY. Buy my matches, mister. They're real cheap.

LEMUEL. No.

OLD LADY. How about some candles; to light your

way, should you get lost.

LEMUEL. Good idea. Get lost.

OLD LADY (pressing on). They're made of genuwine bee's wax. Dip them myself.

LEMUEL (trying to get rid of her). I have important matters that demand my immediate attention . . .

OLD LADY (dovetailing). Come on, mister, I have a lot of grandchildren to support. How about some pot holders? (Holds one up.) Hand-made out of dyed bed sheets and old shirts.

LEMUEL. Where I plan to go, the cooking will be done for me.

OLD LADY. Lucky you. I gotta cook for an army. And growin' kids eat, let me tell you, and food costs money, so come on, mister, how about a bathroom chain?

LEMUEL (his patience wearing thin). No.

OLD LADY. Hand carved busts of lesser known Presidents? Here's one of James Polk.

LEMUEL. No.

OLD LADY. Millard Fillmore? (Grim silence from LEMUEL.) I have a special here on James Garfield. Ran out of carvin' wood for him, so had to use part of a broom handle.

LEMUEL (firmly). Madam, have you ever thought of becoming a sideshow barker at Coney Island?

OLD LADY. No, thanks, I got my pride. (Ever onward.) How about some artificial flowers?

LEMUEL. They make me sneeze!

OLD LADY. Got just the thing -- nose drops made from glycerine and oil of eucalyptus.

LEMUEL. Since I'm not buying those counterfeit posies, I won't need them!

OLD LADY. You'll never have a cold again!

LEMUEL (an exasperated sound). Huh!

OLD LADY. O.K., O.K. (Looks in tray for another item.)

LEMUEL (aside to audience). It's a good thing for her I draw the line at mayhem.

OLD LADY. All right, how about some home-made soap, scented with lilac. (She pushes the soap in his face.)

LEMUEL (inadvertently sniffing the soap; making a face). Ugh!

OLD LADY (briefly checks soap before putting it back). Oh, sorry; that's the disinfectant soap. Now where did I put the . . .

LEMUEL. Madam, I've no need of your tawdry sundries!

OLD LADY (immediately trying a new tack). You know, I had you pegged as a kind-hearted gentleman who'd sympathize with an old Granny having to care for her brood. Mister, I got so many grandchildren, I lost count.

LEMUEL. Well, if you wouldn't have had so many of your own to start with, you wouldn't be complaining now!

OLD LADY. Mister, I have exactly one son, a lazy lout who never left home, who married a prize breeder, and the two of them are figurin' to populate all of New York State. And running that charity ward is wearin' me down!

LEMUEL. I'd throw them out of the house, for I believe charity contaminates both the giver and the receiver . . . So of course you won't want any charity from me.

OLD LADY. Fair enough, but there must be something you could buy. (Brief gesture to tray.) Something you need.

LEMUEL. The only thing I need now is a little bit of luck.

OLD LADY (dollar signs light her eyes). Got just the thing! (Rummages in tray and comes up with a round, transparent disc, about the size of a quarter.) Here -- it's a genuwine four-leaf clover, found it outside of town, up North. See, I covered it with isinglass, so it'll always be with you. (LEMUEL looks at it, for it's not without a certain fascination. And partly out of pity, though pity seldom afflicts him, and partly out of admiration for her perseverance, he relents slightly.)

OLD LADY. Beautiful, ain't it.

LEMUEL (slight pause). I'm not a superstitious man, but I'll take it. How much?

OLD LADY. Only a nickel. (LEMUEL fishes into a pocket with one hand, pulls it closed near his face and opens it. With the other hand he picks a coin which he gives her, returning the first hand to his pocket.) Thank you, sir. (Withholding the clover leaf from him.) And now you have to make a wish.

LEMUEL (what next). A wish?

OLD LADY. Yes, and be careful about it.

LEMUEL. Why should I be careful? I know exactly what I wish!

OLD LADY. O.K. Now say the wish to yourself, so's I can't hear it. (After a disparaging look at her, LEMUEL does so, then a nod in her direction.) Good. That'll be another nickel, please.

LEMUEL. What!

OLD LADY (quickly). Because I found the four-leaf clover, the first wish wouldn't work unless you made it in my presence. The rest are on the house, but this one'll cost you five cents. (More to get rid of her, he angrily gives her his last coin.)

LEMUEL. On the house? Madam, you are a pettifogulating virago who would do well to remain confined in her house, for if I ever see you again . . .

OLD LADY (hastily giving him the clover leaf). Thank you, sir. Rest assured you won't regret the purchase. (Starts going L.) And now, I must be on my way. Pleasure doin' business with you.

LEMUEL. Highway robbery!

OLD LADY (grumbling to herself as she nears exiting). Lordy, what an old person has to do nowadays to make a dime! (She is off L.)

LEMUEL (seething). The predatory harridan has the ethics of a crocodile! (He walks a bit, and calming down, takes out the prisoned clover and looks at it.) Good luck, indeed. Well, it couldn't get any worse. (He returns it to his pocket and mimes walking some more, turning up his collar against the cold.)

(While Lemuel's back is to this area, a section of fence is pushed on extreme R, somewhat front. It is a few feet wide, about seven feet high, and at some clearly visible spot, there's a sign reading "St. Ignatius Church." Possibly a roseate light spills down through the fence, suggesting a stained glass window above and beyond it. LEMUEL turns and comes upon this area unexpectedly.)

LEMUEL (reading sign). "St. Ignatius Church." Well, at least he has a place to stay this winter. (Calling off.) Hey, Iggy, can you get me to Blackwell's Island? (No answer. He shrugs, then glances toward stained glass windows.) Hmm. Funny thing about stained glass windows; they either look good at night from the outside, or during the day from the inside. (A hymn, or anthem, softly played on an organ, is heard from within the church.) The organist must be practicing for Sunday service. (Musing ruefully.) Huh, Lemuel T., when was the last time you saw a stained glass window from the inside of a church? . . . Long ago. Too long ago. (Thinks.) What was that sermon about? . . . Cards -- yes, that life was like a game of cards, with one big difference; that life really spreads the cards out face up -- and the game is in knowing we are free to choose any hand we want . . . (Negatively.) Ah, what did he know, protected in his safe little cocoon. Probably was a rotten poker player anyway. Pick your own cards, indeed. (Seriously.) What did he know about the death of hope, of compromise that invades the empty heart, filling it with base motives and the goals of a park bench bum! (Bitterly.) Card game, indeed! (Wryly argumentative.) Did I pick that headwaitress with a heart as hard as the Queen of Diamonds, or that flowery Queen of Clubs with her sugar plum tears? Did I choose that jaded Queen of Hearts by the millinery shop -- or that weird old Queen of Spades? (An afterthought.) Or, for that matter, that Joker with the umbrella. (The organ continues to play softly.) Actually, if it were a card game, I'd have a full house tonight. A winning hand. (Beginning to get honest with himself.) But what did I win -- nothing but the dreary task of having to face myself. Hah, that can wait till tomorrow. . . . "Your Honor, grant me a reprieve; loan me one more tomorrow, for I've bankrupt all my todays." . . . Oh, where does it all end, Lemuel T.? (The organ music builds in volume imperceptibly.) You were given something this morning, a loan, with no interest required. You were given -- a day, to use, to live in, to be -- of some worth -- in. Once -- I was of some worth. It doesn't seem possible that I could have lost it . . . For somewhere deep inside me, I know that . . . (He has glimpsed something within himself that rekindles his hope.) Is it too late? Maybe not.

(Unknown to LEMUEL, a COP [straight-forward New York type] enters L and remains there watching him.)

LEMUEL. I'm still comparatively young, and I've got my health. (Becoming enthusiastic.) And tonight I know I've got a winning hand -- and I can play the game differently. Why, tomorrow I can go downtown and look for work. Say, there's a fur importer once offered me a position as a driver. I'll look him up and ask him for a job! And for luck, I've got my four-leaf clover. . . (The music, though not loud, is at its highest peak.) I'll be somebody in the world! I'll be of some worth. (The COP moves swiftly to LEMUEL, fixing him with a cold, leveling gaze. The music stops abruptly.)

COP. What are you doing here?

LEMUEL (turning, openly). Nothing.

COP. Where do you live?

LEMUEL. Well, uh -- actually, officer, I'm in the process of moving . . . you see . . .

COP. A drifter, eh?

LEMUEL. Uh -- not exactly ----

COP (firmly). I'm booking you on a vagrancy charge. Put out your hands. (LEMUEL is too stunned to comply, so the COP roughly positions Lemuel's hands and starts to handcuff them.)

LEMUEL (wryly, remembering). Ah, yes -- now I know what the Queen of Spades meant ----

COP (involved with handcuffs, doesn't want any lip). All right.

LEMUEL. Be careful what you wish for -- because you may get it.

COP (finished with handcuffs). You'll have plenty of time to philosophize, I'd say about three months, on Blackwell's Island. (LEMUEL winces.) Now, move along. (As LEMUEL does a long, slow burn, the COP starts leading him off L.)

QUICK CURTAIN OR BLACKOUT

PRODUCTION NOTES

LEMUEL T. THWACKBUSHER (male): Though intelligent and able to attain an aura of dignity sometimes, for the last few years expediency has so ruled his life that he doesn't quite face the fact he's become a park bench bum. (May be played like W. C. Fields, or not.)

HEAD WAITRESS (female): A battle-axe.

SALESLADY (female): Though outside she's encrusted with hard candy, her heart is pure marshmallow.

STREET CLEANER (male, or female with heavy makeup and mustache): A laconic walk-on.

TOUGH BOY (male or female): Gritty.

MAN WITH UMBRELLA (male): A gentleman to the core.

MOTHER (female): A self-righteous bulwark.

LITTLE GIRL (female): Just this side of being a brat.

TWO WOMEN (female): Allies of the mother.

FLORABELLE (female): Her life is one long sybaritic sail on Cleopatra's barge, down the Hudson. (May be played like Mae West, or not.)

OLD LADY (female): A plucky crone whom poverty has made indefatigably resourceful and persistent.

COP(S) (male): The actor plays five different policemen; his acting, makeup and suggested accents should evoke five distinctive characterizations. (If desired, five men could play these roles.)

(NOTE: If a smaller cast is desired, the women could double on their parts.)

COSTUMES:

They should suggest the first decade of the 20th Century, simply or ornately, as desired.

LEMUEL: Hat, shirt and tie, jacket, pants, shoes and socks, which are all the worst for wear.
HEAD WAITRESS: Severe blouse, three-quarter jacket and long skirt; possibly wears glasses.
SALESLADY: Blouse and long skirt; may wear pince-nez.
TOUGH BOY: Fairly oversized cap, moth-eaten sweater and knickers.
MOTHER, LITTLE GIRL and TWO WOMEN: Dressed well-to-do.
FLORABELLE: Georgeously attired, possibly a three-quarter cape over an elegant dress which accents her curvaceous figure; could wear a large picture hat with feathers or flowers.
OLD LADY: Shrouded from head to toe in an amorphous, all-covering, cape-like garment.
COP(S): Police hat, uniform and billy club.

SET:

No set is required for this play, since area staging is utilized throughout. The few simply constructed (or borrowed) set pieces that will be needed are:

1) A park bench (or a simple box-like thing suggesting one) equipped with rolling casters so one person can slide it off stage with ease.
2) A counter (few feet wide) with casters.

3) The skeletal outline of a shop window (perhaps five feet wide and seven feet high) also with casters, which is pushed on and off stage by a connected pole.
4) A stand sign reading "Trolley Stop."
5) A section of fence, about seven feet high, a few feet wide, with a sign reading "St. Ignatius Church."

PROPERTIES:

Apart from the set pieces listed above, the following properties are needed:

Autumn leaves and newspaper for park bench.

LEMUEL: Two short cigar butts, two toothpicks and wooden matches, one newspaper sheet.

HEAD WAITRESS: Reservation tablet, pencil,and a fairly tall plotted plant (plastic will do).

SALESLADY: A variety of candy boxes, lapel or pendant watch, handkerchief and large red bow.

STREET CLEANER: Street-cleaning broom and two-wheeled trash cart (disguised two-wheel tote cart will do).

TOUGH BOY: Ball.

MAN: Umbrella, newspaper.

OLD LADY: A hand-held tray (with a supporting strap that loops around the neck) containing match boxes, candles, pot holders, bathroom chain, three small busts of men (painted dark to look like hand-carved wooden figurines), artificial flowers, soap, and a round transparent (plastic) disc inside which there is a (painted) four-leaf clover.

COP: Billy club, handcuffs.

CHART OF STAGE POSITIONS

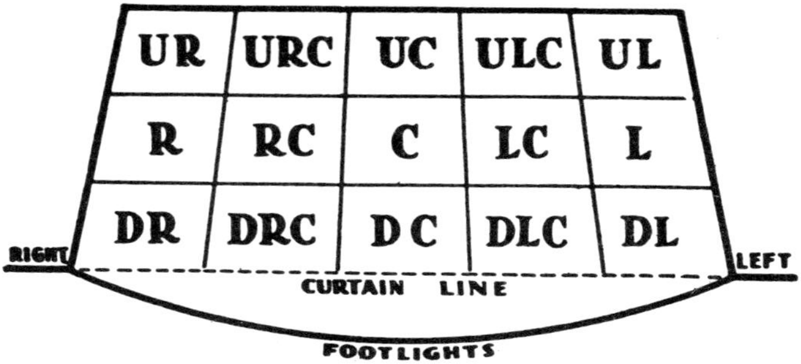

STAGE POSITIONS

Upstage means away from the footlights, *downstage* means toward the footlights, and *right* and *left* are used with reference to the actor as he faces the audience. R means *right,* L means *left,* U means *up,* D means *down,* C means *center,* and these abbreviations are used in combination, as: U R for *up right,* R C for *right center,* D L C for *down left center,* etc. A territory designated on the stage refers to a general area, rather than to a given point.

NOTE: Before starting rehearsals, chalk off your stage or rehearsal space as indicated above in the *Chart of Stage Positions.* Then teach your actors the meanings and positions of these fundamental terms of stage movement by having them walk from one position to another until they are familiar with them. The use of these abbreviated terms in directing the play saves time, speeds up rehearsals, and reduces the amount of explanation the director has to give to his actors.

DIRECTOR'S NOTES

DIRECTOR'S NOTES

DIRECTOR'S NOTES

DIRECTOR'S NOTES